A TRUE BOOK

SPACE EXPLORATION

MARS ROVERS

Jessica Cohn

Children's Press®
An imprint of Scholastic Inc.

Content Consultant
Roger D. Launius, PhD
Former Chief Historian, NASA

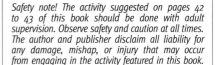

Library of Congress Cataloging-in-Publication Data

Names: Cohn, Jessica, author.

Title: Mars rovers/Jessica Cohn.

Other titles: True book.

Description: First edition. | New York, NY: Children's Press, an imprint of Scholastic Inc., 2022. | Series: A true book | Includes bibliographical references and index. | Audience: Ages 8–10. | Audience: Grades 4–6. | Summary: "A new set of True Books on Space Exploration"—Provided by publisher.

Identifiers: LCCN 2021041671 (print) | LCCN 2021041672 (ebook) | ISBN 9781338825886 (library binding) | ISBN 9781338825893 (paperback) | ISBN 9781338825909 (ebk)

Subjects: LCSH: Roving vehicles (Astronautics)—Juvenile literature. | Mars (Planet)—Exploration—Equipment and supplies—Juvenile literature.

Classification: LCC TL795 .C65 2022 (print) | LCC TL795 (ebook) | DDC 629.2/95099923—dc23

LC record available at https://lccn.loc.gov/2021041671

LC ebook record available at https://lccn.loc.gov/2021041672

10 9 8 7 6 5 4 3 2 1   22 23 24 25 26

Printed in the U.S.A. 113
First edition, 2022

Design by Kathleen Petelinsek
Series produced by Spooky Cheetah Press

Front cover: An artist's rendering of Perseverance exploring the surface of Mars

Back cover: The Ingenuity helicopter flying on Mars

Find the Truth!

Everything you are about to read is true *except* for one of the sentences on this page.

Which one is **TRUE**?

T or F   Multiple missions to Mars have failed.

T or F   The Red Planet rovers keep getting smaller.

Find the answers in this book.

What's in This Book?

Perseverance touches down on Mars.

MOXIE has the ability to create oxygen on Mars.

The **BIG** Truth

Is Life on Mars Possible?

4 The Search for Meaning

Ingenuity takes flight on Mars.

Getting to Know Our Neighbor

Among the **eight planets** in our solar system, **Mars** is the fourth closest to the sun, right after Earth. Mars, our planetary neighbor, is about half the size of our planet. We sometimes see Mars in the night sky. It may also appear in early morning as a **glowing red dot**. In fact, Mars got its nickname, the Red Planet, from its reddish appearance. Humans have wondered for ages whether Mars has enough water to support life. Photos of the planet showed that its polar ice caps contain frozen water. We also know that the Red Planet, because of its distance from the sun, is super cold! But there is so much more to discover. **Could life survive there?** Our Red Planet rovers, special vehicles designed to drive over rough terrain, have the job of answering our questions about this **fascinating planet**.

Some rovers have been powered by solar panels. Others, including Perseverance, use nuclear batteries.

Perseverance means "steady effort to achieve something difficult."

Learning from Rovers

Perseverance is the latest U.S. rover to explore Mars. It landed on the Red Planet in February 2021, nearly seven months after it was launched. The National Aeronautics and Space Administration (NASA) is the U.S. government agency in charge of space and airplane science. To build Perseverance, thousands of NASA workers put in decades of effort, fine-tuning how rovers are built. They built on what they learned from each mission that came before.

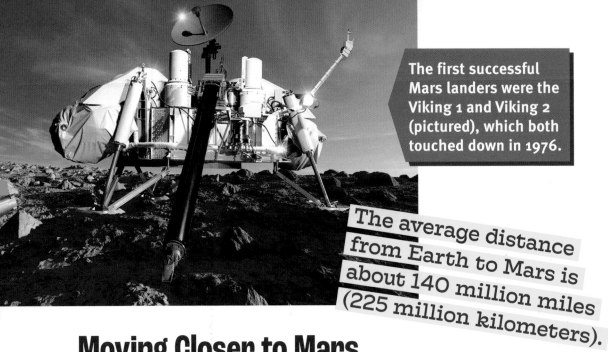

The first successful Mars landers were the Viking 1 and Viking 2 (pictured), which both touched down in 1976.

The average distance from Earth to Mars is about 140 million miles (225 million kilometers).

Moving Closer to Mars

The first spacecraft to successfully reach Mars flew past the planet in 1965. Next, NASA sent instruments to orbit, or circle, the planet and explore its **atmosphere**. To look more closely at Mars, they then built machines that could reach the surface, called landers.

The first successful landers were sent in the 1970s. Heat shields protected the landers as they entered the Martian atmosphere. Then parachutes opened to help guide them downward.

Red Planet Rovers

Unlike landers, which stay in place, rovers can move across a planet's surface. The first successful Mars rover was Sojourner, which landed in 1997, on the Fourth of July. It was the size of a microwave oven.

Sojourner touched down inside a lander that was shaped like a pyramid and covered with airbags. On touchdown, the lander bounced for several minutes. When it settled, a hatch opened, and Sojourner moved out onto the surface. The lander remained in place to collect weather information.

Airbags

Opened pyramid

Sojourner operated for 92 sols, or Martian days.

An average Martian sol lasts 24 hours, 39 minutes, and 35 seconds. That's about 40 minutes longer than a day and night on Earth.

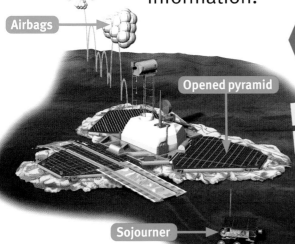
Sojourner

Under the Martian Sun

Sojourner's job was to look for signs of water, to determine whether Mars could support life. Living things on Earth need water to survive.

Sojourner and its lander used special radios to communicate with Earth. They went silent toward the end of September 1997—a little more than two months after landing. This successful mission allowed Sojourner's cameras to send more than 550 amazing images. What's more, the rover studied ancient rocks and found evidence that water affected its formation. This meant it was possible there were simple life-forms on Mars long ago.

Sojourner, the first rover to operate on Mars, was sent to a flat area so the wheels could work.

Sojourner means "temporary visitor."

The Twin Rovers

Opportunity's mission was planned to last 90 days, but it lasted more than 14 years!

Next, NASA sent a pair of twin rovers to look for signs of water. Spirit landed on January 3, 2004. Opportunity followed on January 24.

The twins explored opposite sides of Mars, in flat areas that looked like they could have been formed by water.

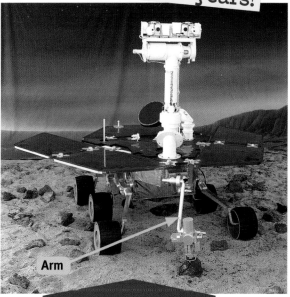

Arm

The small arm on each of the twin rovers was for using tools.

Each rover was the size of a golf cart and carried more equipment than Sojourner did, including advanced tools to scratch below the surface. Their cameras beamed hundreds of thousands of images to an orbiter, which sent the images to Earth.

Opportunity traveled more than 28 miles (45 km), setting a record for distance covered on another planet.

Spirit's solar panels were completely covered in dust by the end of its mission.

More Proof

When water interacts with materials in rock, the water changes it. So Opportunity and Spirit studied ancient rocks on Mars, looking for signs of water activity. They found evidence that long ago there was water inside the ground and flowing on the surface of Mars.

Spirit went silent in March 2010. And NASA lost communication with Opportunity in June 2018. But the twins' tests proved that Mars was wetter long ago, making it more likely that the planet had hosted life.

Teamwork!

Space exploration projects cost billions of dollars. More than 70 governments around the world have space agencies, which often work in cooperation to share costs—and knowledge. These are the five most active agencies around the world:

1. NASA: National Aeronautics and Space Administration (U.S.)
2. CNSA: China National Space Administration
3. ESA: European Space Agency
4. Roscosmos: Russian Federal Space Agency
5. ISRO: Indian Space Research Organisation

Source: RankRed.com 2021, ranked for achievements, abilities, and budgets

The International Space Station—a science lab in outer space—is supported by 15 nations.

Curiosity has 17 cameras and an arm that can take selfies.

Martian rock and soil have locked-in gases from the atmosphere. Studying the rocks and soil helps scientists think about the environment in which those gases formed.

Curiosity Proves Itself

NASA's next Mars rover, Curiosity, landed on August 6, 2012. Unlike previous rovers, it didn't bounce around on the surface in a lander covered with airbags. Instead, the landing system fired rockets that allowed the lander to hover above the surface and lower the rover on cables.

Curiosity's large tool kit is capable of advanced testing. It has a 7-foot (2-meter) arm and a laser to zap rocks. Its mission: to look for further evidence of ancient water sources and possible life.

Curiosity has a formal name too: the Mars Science Laboratory.

Curiosity weighs 2,000 pounds (907 kilograms) and is 10 feet (3 m) long.

Curiosity Gets Serious

Since landing, Curiosity has explored an ancient riverbed, taking samples of rock, soil, and air to analyze on board. It has found traces of **organics**, which are materials that could have served as food for **microorganisms**. The clues Curiosity has found suggest there were wet conditions on Mars more than once. This makes it even more likely that Mars was habitable, or life-supporting, in the past. Curiosity has been working so well that Perseverance was built like it.

Mars Rover Landing Sites

Rovers have been sent to explore different areas of the Red Planet. The first five successful rovers were built by NASA. The sixth, Zhurong, was sent by China.

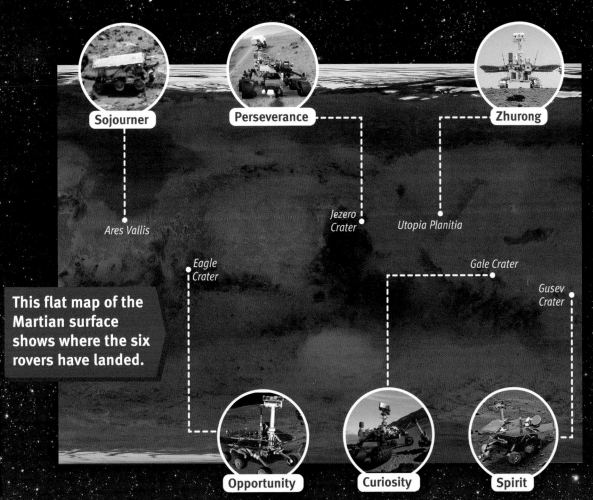

Sojourner

Perseverance

Zhurong

Ares Vallis

Jezero Crater

Utopia Planitia

Eagle Crater

Gale Crater

Gusev Crater

This flat map of the Martian surface shows where the six rovers have landed.

Opportunity

Curiosity

Spirit

This illustration shows what happened in the final stages of Perseverance's descent and landing on February 18, 2021.

Buildings in New York, Chicago, Los Angeles, and other cities lit up with red lights to celebrate Perseverance's landing.

Perseverance on Mars

Perseverance launched in July 2020, riding a tall Atlas rocket, which dropped away after liftoff. The rover traveled 293 million miles (472 million km) to get to its landing spot. A shield and shell protected Perseverance as it sped through space. Before touchdown, the landing system fired up rockets to slow down, as happened during Curiosity's descent. Perseverance dropped down on cables. When its wheels sensed the ground, the rover cut itself loose.

This photo, taken from a Mars orbiter, shows the Jezero Crater, where Perseverance touched down.

Trip Planner

Perseverance, which is the size of a small SUV, is NASA's largest Mars rover to date. And it is the first that can take note of its surroundings and avoid obstacles as it drives. The rover has instruments that operate as eyes and ears, and computers that work like brains. Perseverance also has maps stored in its memory that help it navigate.

Seven Minutes of Terror!

The final stage of a spacecraft's landing is known as Entry, Descent, and Landing (EDL). At NASA, a Mars EDL is known as "seven minutes of terror." That is the point at which about half of all missions fail. A lack of communication adds to the tension. It takes 11 minutes for radio transmissions from Mars to reach Earth. The team at Mission Control has no idea whether the rover landed safely until it has already touched down—or not—on the planet.

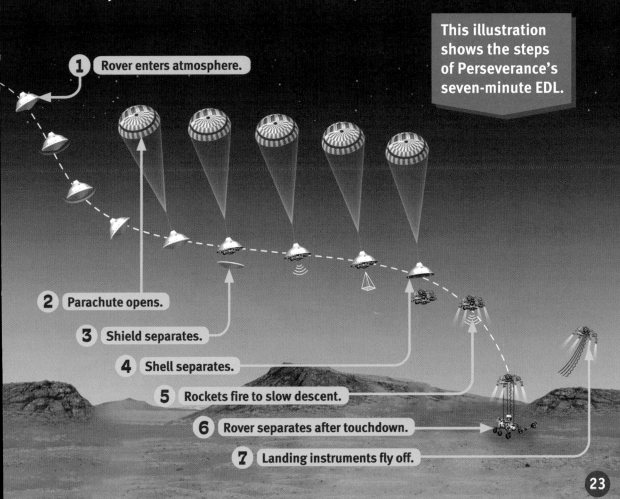

This illustration shows the steps of Perseverance's seven-minute EDL.

1 Rover enters atmosphere.

2 Parachute opens.

3 Shield separates.

4 Shell separates.

5 Rockets fire to slow descent.

6 Rover separates after touchdown.

7 Landing instruments fly off.

The Sidekick

Perseverance is not alone. Ingenuity, a helicopter, is its partner. The tiny aircraft rode to Mars in the rover's belly and exited after touchdown. Two months later, Ingenuity lifted off and climbed 10 feet (3 m). This took plenty of planning because the Martian atmosphere is very thin. Rotating blades push air down to create the "lift" a helicopter needs to fly. A helicopter couldn't fly on the moon, for example, because the moon has no atmosphere. Ingenuity had to be super lightweight. Its blades had to spin extra fast.

Ingenuity weighs less than 4 pounds (1.8 kg) on Earth. Because Mars has less **gravity**, Ingenuity weighs 1.5 pounds (0.68 kg) there.

The helicopter has a camera. Its images help determine its flight position.

Eyes in the Sky

Ingenuity's achievement was historic. The initial 40-second flight marked the first time a robotic instrument lifted off from Mars. It was the first-ever controlled flight on another planet!

Since then, the solar-powered helicopter has worked as a scout. Ingenuity checks out places that Perseverance can go and takes images of possible paths from above. The helicopter has performed so well that NASA plans to build flyers like it for future missions.

Perseverance uses lasers to study the planet's surface.

One Very Special Rover

Perseverance has a computer that acts as a driver, making it the first rover that does not have to follow commands from Earth. It is also the first rover with microphones, which captured the first Martian sounds. By recording sounds as it zaps rocks with its advanced laser, the rover helps scientists figure out what the rocks are made of.

Making Oxygen

The rover also carries an experimental device, called MOXIE, for making oxygen. The Martian atmosphere is 95 percent **carbon dioxide**. MOXIE splits carbon dioxide into the parts, or elements, that make it up. In the process, it creates oxygen. Whenever something burns, what's burning is oxygen. Being able to generate oxygen on Mars may make it easier for future missions to burn fuel to return spacecraft to Earth.

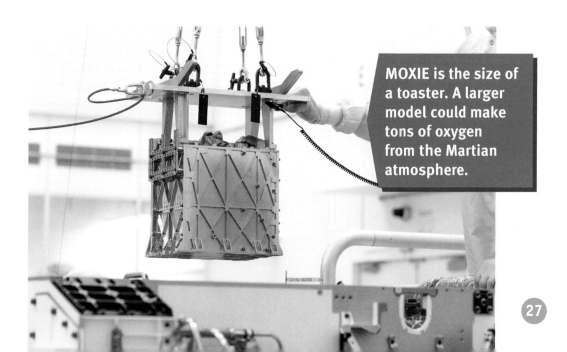

MOXIE is the size of a toaster. A larger model could make tons of oxygen from the Martian atmosphere.

The Mission

With the help of Ingenuity, Perseverance is exploring a bowl-shaped crater about 28 miles (45 km) wide. NASA scientists hope to find traces of ancient life within the exploration area. The rover has instruments in its belly that take samples of surface materials. On the bottom of the rover, there is an advanced set of drill bits arranged like a carousel. This drilling instrument rotates like a wheel.

Timeline of Mars Rover Missions

NOVEMBER 1971
The Soviet Union (Russia) sends two rovers to Mars, but both are unsuccessful.

JULY 1997
The Mars Pathfinder mission successfully delivers Sojourner.

JANUARY 2004
The Mars Exploration Rover mission lands twin rovers, Opportunity and Spirit.

What's in Store

The rover's big arm reaches out to drill rock. A small arm from the belly picks the samples up and moves them into tubes. Like the rovers that came before, this rover will not be returned to Earth. Instead, Perseverance is storing rocks and soil for later missions to retrieve. To store the samples, the rover fills and seals tubes that it leaves near landmarks. It maps the spots.

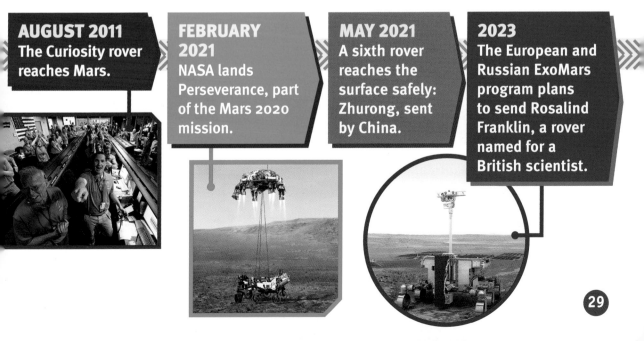

AUGUST 2011
The Curiosity rover reaches Mars.

FEBRUARY 2021
NASA lands Perseverance, part of the Mars 2020 mission.

MAY 2021
A sixth rover reaches the surface safely: Zhurong, sent by China.

2023
The European and Russian ExoMars program plans to send Rosalind Franklin, a rover named for a British scientist.

Is Life on Mars Possible?

For decades, humans have wondered if we will ever be able to live on Mars. Many obstacles would have to be overcome to make that happen. Experts at NASA continue to explore possible solutions to these obstacles.

Obstacle: Strong Solar Radiation

Mars does not have a **magnetic field** like Earth's for protection from the sun's **radiation**.

Possible Solution:

Companies are working to develop homes that could withstand such radiation.

Concept home on Mars

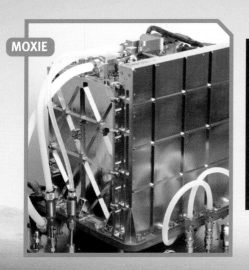
MOXIE

Obstacle: Lack of Oxygen

We need oxygen to breathe. But the Mars atmosphere is only 0.16 percent oxygen.

Possible Solution: With a device like MOXIE, oxygen can be separated from the carbon dioxide in the atmosphere. It might then be concentrated for use by humans.

Obstacle: People Need Water

There is no surface water on the Red Planet.

Possible Solution:

NASA is developing technologies that can take water from below the Martian soil.

Concept water drill

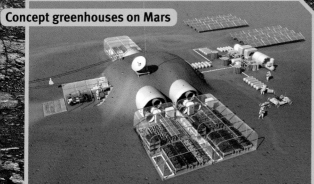
Concept greenhouses on Mars

Obstacle: Lack of Food

There are no plants or animals that can be used for food.

Possible Solution:

NASA is experimenting with crops that could grow in greenhouses made for Mars.

31

Jezero Crater, where Perseverance roams, was wet 3.5 billion years ago.

This illustration shows how water would have covered Jezero Crater.

The Search for Meaning

Long ago the atmosphere of Mars was thicker and warmer, but the surface is a cold desert now. Windstorms are common, and rust-colored dust can circle the planet. But the rovers have found signs of former lakes, and there is evidence that rivers flowed long ago, as well. By testing rock and soil samples to see how old they are and where they came from, scientists can better understand when and how long Mars was warmer and wetter.

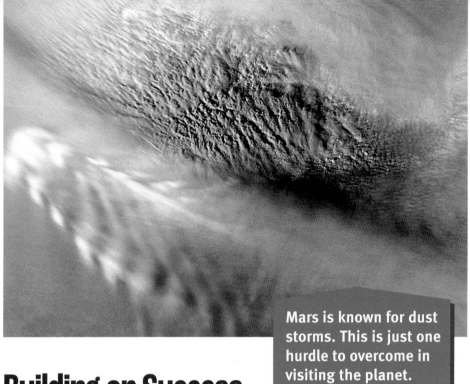

Mars is known for dust storms. This is just one hurdle to overcome in visiting the planet.

Building on Success

Multiple Mars missions have missed the planet or failed during touchdown, yet scientists believe the efforts are worth it because we learn from failure. There is a chance Perseverance will not find the signs of life it is looking for. But the mission succeeded just by avoiding a crash landing and getting Ingenuity to fly. Now the rover's testing helps us better understand not just Mars but rocky planets in general.

Mars Missions

NASA has several Mars missions running at the same time as the rovers. Orbiters watch Mars from above and Landers study one area of the planet's surface.

Spacecraft	Launched In . . .	Job
Mars Odyssey Orbiter	2001	Detects water and buried ice on Mars and studies radiation
Mars Reconnaissance Orbiter	2005	Studies the planet's **geology** and **climate**
Maven Orbiter	2013	Studies the Martian atmosphere and relays data from the rovers
Insight Lander	2018	Measures the planet's core, or center

The team at NASA's Jet Propulsion Laboratory celebrates a successful landing.

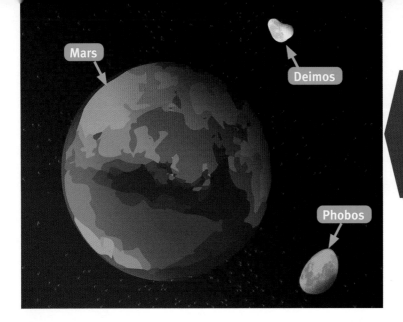

Mars

Deimos

Phobos

Japan has plans to send a rover to Phobos, one of the two Martian moons (shown here), to collect samples.

New Goals

The first Mars rovers were tasked with finding signs of water beyond the icy caps. Now rovers are investigating the Martian climate and geology in depth. Data gathered by rovers and other instruments show that carbon dioxide around Mars has lessened over time. As we figure out how the gas disappeared and what formed instead, we may find ways to deal with increased carbon dioxide in Earth's atmosphere. This may lead to ideas about how to combat **climate change** on Earth.

The Practice Fields

Astrobiology is the study of life throughout the universe. Astrobiologists analyze the rovers' data to address big questions: How do rocky planets like ours form and change? Can Mars host human life?

To prepare for future missions to Mars, scientists test equipment and personal gear in the harshest locations on Earth. They run tests in deserts, oceans, and volcanoes. Someday humans will go to the Red Planet, instead of only robots. NASA is getting ready!

Tools that will be used on Mars are tested in the Atacama Desert in Chile.

The Atacama Desert is thought of as Mars-like mainly because it is the driest place on Earth.

This is Perseverance's first selfie. It took about a dozen Earthling scientists one week to plan it out.

Scientists have been studying which foods might grow in Mars-like conditions. Successful crops include carrots, onions, dandelions, and lettuce.

Yet to Come

The rovers have given us a closer look at Mars, and there is more coming! Future missions have plans to further study the interior of the Red Planet. NASA is finding ways to speed communication using lasers. Scientists are also designing rovers that will double as homes for humans.

Becoming Martians

NASA teams complete tasks that once seemed futuristic. In just over 50 years, humans progressed from accomplishing the first Mars flyby to being able to fly a helicopter on the planet. Everything scientists learn about the Red Planet makes it more likely that humans will get there in person one day. We no longer simply search for water on Mars. Now we explore the possibility of living there.

This is an artist's concept illustration of a Martian city.

Tracking Martian Temperatures

Rovers collect data that enable scientists at NASA to better understand Mars. They might study changes in temperature or the makeup of rocks or the atmosphere. This graph shows temperatures that Curiosity recorded on the Red Planet. It tracks changes in ground and air temperature over two sols, or Martian days. Study the graph and answer the questions that follow.

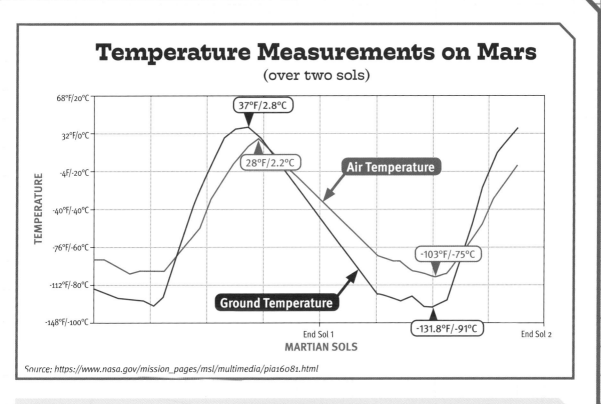

Temperature Measurements on Mars
(over two sols)

Source: https://www.nasa.gov/mission_pages/msl/multimedia/pia16081.html

Analyze It!

1 What was the lowest ground temperature recorded?

2 What was the highest air temperature recorded?

3 Which temperature range (air or ground) was more extreme?

4 Compare the two ranges and describe a similarity in their patterns. Explain how the ranges on Mars are similar to day and night temperatures on Earth, using what you know about Earth and what you just read about Mars.

ANSWERS: 1. -131°F/-91°C. 2. 28°F/2.2°C. 3. Ground temperature. 4. Air and ground temperatures increase and decrease at the same time. This is similar to the way temperature changes on Earth throughout the day and night.

Life Signs

NASA is looking for signs of life in Martian soil. Living things breathe and eat. Breathing can be identified by the release of small bubbles of CO_2 gas. Eating can be identified by an increase in temperature. See if you can find the living thing in this activity!

Directions

1 Label the cups A, B, C, and D. Add 4 tablespoons sand and 1 teaspoon sugar to each cup.

Materials

Paper and marker
Four paper cups
Tablespoon and teaspoon
Sand
Sugar
Salt
Antacid tablet (fizzing type)
Yeast
Gelatin powder
Hot water

4 Take notes on what you see and feel when holding the cups. Only one is showing true signs of life. Which one, and why?

2 Add 1 teaspoon salt to cup A, 1 teaspoon antacid to cup B, 1 teaspoon yeast to cup C, and 1 teaspoon gelatin to cup D.

ASK AN ADULT FOR HELP

3 Mix the contents of each cup. Ask an adult to add just enough hot water to each cup to cover the mixture.

Check Your Results

The mixture in cup C is releasing bubbles of CO_2 gas and also getting warmer. That's because yeast is a living fungus. It is eating the sugar in the cup and breathing. The mixture in cup B is releasing gas bubbles, but that is just a chemical reaction. The lack of heat shows that the antacid tablet is not a living thing. The other two cups don't show any signs of life.

True Statistics

Sojourner's top speed: 2 feet (0.6 m) per minute

Days Opportunity lasted: 5,110 sols (5,250 days)

Diameter of Curiosity's wheels: 20 inches (50.8 cm)

Perseverance's weight on Earth: 2,260 pounds (1,025 kg)

Percentage of carbon dioxide in Martian atmosphere: 95%

Martian surface gravity: 38% of Earth's

Length of Martian sol: 24 hours and 39 minutes and 35 seconds

Length of Earth day: 24 hours

Length of Martian orbit around sun: 687 days, or 1.88 Earth years

Length of Earth's orbit around sun: 365 days, 1 year

Did you find the truth?

T Multiple missions to Mars have failed.

F The Red Planet rovers keep getting smaller.

Resources

Other books in this series:

 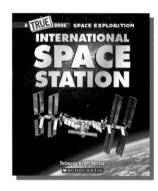 

You can also look at:

Aldrin, Buzz, and Marianne Dyson. *Welcome to Mars: Making a Home on the Red Planet*. Washington, D.C.: National Geographic Society, 2015.

Bizony, Piers. *NASA Missions to Mars: A Visual History of Our Quest to Explore the Red Planet*. Beverly, MA: Motorbooks, 2022.

Woolf, Alex. *The Science of Spacecraft: The Cosmic Truth About Rockets, Satellites, and Probes*. New York: Scholastic, 2019.

Glossary

atmosphere (AT-muhs-feer) the mixture of gases that surrounds a planet

carbon dioxide (KAHR-buhn dye-AHK-side) a gas that is a mixture of carbon and oxygen, with no color or odor

climate (KLYE-mit) the weather typical of a place over a long period of time

climate change (KLYE-mit CHAYNJ) global warming and other changes in the weather and weather patterns that are happening because of human activity

geology (jee-AH-luh-jee) the study of a planet's physical structure, especially its layers of soil and rock

gravity (GRAV-i-tee) the force that pulls things toward the center of the earth and keeps them from floating away

magnetic field (mag-NET-ik FEELD) the region around a magnetic material, electric current, or body in space that has the power to attract metals or move electrical charges

microorganisms (MYE-kroh-OR-guh-niz-uhms) tiny living things, some of which cause sickness but others needed to stay healthy

organics (or-GAN-iks) materials from or produced by living things

radiation (RAY-dee-AY-shuhn) energy given off in the form of light or heat

Index

Page numbers in **bold** indicate illustrations.

About the Author

Jessica Cohn is the author of more than 60 nonfiction books. She has a master of science in written communications and decades of experience in educational publishing. NASA is on a mission to keep people up-to-date on exciting developments, and the agency's extensive site helped the author find the newest facts. Cohn encourages you to visit nasa.gov to see videos of Mars exploration and updates on the rovers and other spacecraft for yourself. There's nothing like it!